T0113592

## Author's Published Works

*Quotes & Inspirational*

Purple Pieces

*Novels*

Every "I Love You" Isn't True
Every "I Love You" Isn't True
Part 2

# PURPLE
# PIECES
## VOLUME II

Inspirational Quotes & Sayings

RaSheeda Bryant-McNeil

**author**HOUSE®

AuthorHouse™
1663 Liberty Drive
Bloomington, IN 47403
www.authorhouse.com
Phone: 833-262-8899

Published by AuthorHouse 01/20/2022

ISBN: 978-1-6655-4985-1 (sc)
ISBN: 978-1-6655-4986-8 (e)

Library of Congress Control Number: 2013918021

Print information available on the last page.

*"Take the pressure off yourself and put pressure on the word"*
*(Janice Thomas).*

# Dedication Page

To all of the **Janice Thomas'** in the world
who unselfishly take time out of their schedule
to pour unto others expecting nothing,
but for God to get all the glory.

# 1

*Stay away from friends who only want to show you that they have money and appreciate the friends that show you how to get money.*

# 2

*In order to move on you have to want your peace greater than you want their presence.*

**3**

*After something expires it is no longer good for you and I'm not referring to food.*

# *4*

*Even the best fruit cannot be eaten if picked too soon.*

# 5

*Pride will always be the longest distance between two people, so ask yourself, "do you want to be happy or do you want to be right?"*

# 6

## *When a woman leaves you for herself she won't be back.*

# 7

*Stick to the plan even when
the person you planned
it with switches up.*

# 8

*Temporary people will teach you
your most permanent lessons.*

# 9

*Distance yourself from people who bring out who you don't want to be anymore.*

# *10*

*Don't let people call you only when they are down because you had the same number when they were up. .*

# 11

*Some people are throwing away friendships for enemies who are pretending to be their friend.*

# *12*

*People who pick unnecessary battles are really at war within themselves.*

# 13

*Remember that everything that settles is at the bottom. Stay top shelf.*

# *14*

## *Asking more than once is too close to begging.*

# 15

*Be careful how you treat people because Karma doesn't wait anymore.*

# 16

*You cannot train a fire not to burn you.*

# 17

*Blood is thicker than water but peace of mind outranks them both.*

# 18

*You don't always have to tell your side of the story. Time will tell it.*

# 19

*Don't go into battle for someone who wouldn't even care if you died on the battlefield.*

# 20

*Never change sides. Just
change lanes and realize
everyone isn't loyal.*

# *21*

*God will replace the one
who misplaced you with
someone better.*

## 22

*There is no competition when you have already won. The only person you should try to be better than is the person you were yesterday.*

# 23

*You cannot place a dollar sign on trust nor loyalty.*

# 24

*Regarding relationships: Rule number 1... don't be number 2.*

# 25

*The devil will tell you a lie in your own voice. Don't believe him.*

# 26

*Worrying profits you nothing.*

# 27

*Worrying only increases in the negative while faith will only increase in the positive.*

# 28

*You don't have to raise your standards. Just know that I'm not lowering mine.*

# **29**

*Energy in the positive
is better well spent.*

# 30

*A loss will stop feeling like a loss when you find something better.*

# *31*

*When it's all said and done most of the time who you thought you loss really loss you.*

# 32

*Never let anything
temporary hinder what
you know is permanent.*

# 33

*Although the other person may be wrong you still have to see the truth about yourself in the situation. You will either see how you contributed to it or the reason you accepted it in the first place.*

# 34

*Low self-esteem will make you stay, knowing your mate only wants to play.*

# 35

*If you are giving your all and it is still not good enough, stop giving it.*

# 36

*Your grind has to be personal. If it isn't then you are not really grinding.*

# 37

*When you know who you
are it does not matter what
they call you. It only matters
what you answer to.*

# 38

*A person worth fighting
for will never put you in
position where you have to.*

# 39

*Do not let the bad distort
your image of what is good.*

# *40*

## *The enemy can never win until you give up.*

# 41

## *Love to learn and learn to love*

# 42

*Learn yourself first so that you can teach others how to love you.*

# 43

*A mother can never be a father and a father can never be a mother.*

## 44

*One of the best things a
mother can teach her son is
how to treat a woman.*

# 45

*One of the best things a mother can teach her daughter is how to be a woman.*

# *46*

*One of the best things a father can do is teach his son how to be a man.*

# *47*

*One of the best things a father can teach his daughter is how to recognize a good man.*

# *48*

*One of the greatest gifts a child can give a parent is to be better than them.*

# 49

*Your goal as a parent is not for your child to be you but to be better than you.*

# 50

*Teach your children not only
to expect love from others
but to be love to others.*

# 51

*Your child's laugh is the sweetest sound you will ever hear.*

# 52

*During a divorce love
your children more than
you hate one another.*

# 53

*Your first goal should be
to complete your goals.*

## *54*

*If it is a distraction cut it off.*

# 55

*The world is changing.
No one said you have to
accept it, just respect it.*

# 56

*Understand when you open the door to tell someone what to do in their household, you open the door for someone to tell you what to do in yours.*

# 57

*Communication is key, trust is the foundation, loyalty is the bridge, and love is the result.*

# 58

*Be who you want to be with.*

# 59

*You get what you put out or you eventually get left out.*

# 60

*Please do not be the one that never brings anything to the "table" but always want to eat. Eventually, people will stop inviting you.*

# 61

*Love yourself enough to walk away from anyone that has proven they do not love you.*

# 62

*Appreciate your now and you will be happier later.*

# 63

*"I'm sorry" never touches the
heart without sincerity.*

# 64

*You don't have to be asleep*
*to not be awake.*

# 65

*Love who you are
unapologetically.*

# 66

*Some people need an audience.
You have to let people be
legends in their own mind.*

# 67

*Sometimes what you need is
to avoid what you want.*

# 68

*Don't lose your blessing trying to treat people how they treat you. It's not about them.*

# 69

*Let truth go before anger
or the truth will probably
never be heard.*

# 70

*The best advice I was ever given was to listen to my elders.*

# 71

*Some of you are anointed for what others have to be qualified for. Don't let people make you feel bad about your gift.*

# 72

*Prayer is included in my business plans because no one can do it like God can.*

# 73

*Whatever you lose in life*
*don't lose yourself.*

# 74

*Your kids deserve to see you
in peace and not in pieces.*

# 75

*For those of you raised purely on love be careful with those who were raised solely on survival. They will bite the hand that tried to feed them because they are too traumatized to realize that they were being fed ... in love.*

# 76

*Everyone in your life at some point is going to hurt you. You just have to decide which one you're going to let go of.... the pain or the person.*

# 77

*If you are always solid when a
situation folds you never have
to worry if it was them or you.*

# 78

*If you don't let the past die
it will never let you live.*

# 79

*Godfidence is knowing that when God is for you who can be against you.*

# *80*

## *Always be authentically you - unapologetically.*

# Notes:

_____
_____
_____
_____
_____
_____
_____
_____
_____
_____
_____
_____
_____
_____
_____
_____
_____
_____

# *Acknowledgments*

*to*

*others who have poured into me*
Pastor Charonn Barnette (House
of Restoration Ministries)
Pastor Joseph Graham (Road to
Damascus Christian Church)
Mr. Larry Quick Sr.
Ms. Naomi Jackson

&

my Godmother who was full of wisdom
**Beverly Ottis** (R.I.H.)

Printed in the United States
by Baker & Taylor Publisher Services